S'more Cookbook

Tasty Creative S'more Recipes

BY

Stephanie Sharp

Copyright © 2019 by Stephanie Sharp

wwwwwwwwwwwwwwwwwwwwwwwwwwwwwwwwwwww

License Notes

Copyright 2019 by Stephanie Sharp All rights reserved.

No part of this Book may be transmitted or reproduced into any format for any means without the proper permission of the Author. This includes electronic or mechanical methods, photocopying or printing.

The Reader assumes all risk when following any of the guidelines or ideas written as they are purely suggestion and for informational purposes. The Author has taken every precaution to ensure accuracy of the work but bears no responsibility if damages occur due to a misinterpretation of suggestions.

wwwwwwwwwwwwwwwwwwwwwwwwwwwwwwwwwwww

My deepest thanks for buying my book! Now that you have made this investment in time and money, you are now eligible for free e-books on a weekly basis! Once you subscribe by filling in the box below with your email address, you will start to receive free and discounted book offers for unique and informative books. There is nothing more to do! A reminder email will be sent to you a few days before the promotion expires so you will never have to worry about missing out on this amazing deal. Enter your email address below to get started. Thanks again for your purchase!

Just visit the link or scan QR-code to get started!

https://stephanie-sharp.subscribemenow.com

wwwwwwwwwwwwwwwwwwwwwwwwwwwwwwwww

Table of Contents

Introduction

S'mores are a classic family night-time treat that most are accustom to. All that's needed is a Campfire, Family and Friends, and of course Chocolate, Graham Crackersd and Marshmallow. As simple as these ingredients are, they make a delicious treat that will leave you satisfied. In this S'mores book, there are 30 delicious smore recipes that you never imagined could be made with S'mores and they are the best recipes ever!

Golden Graham S'mores Squares

These crispy treats bind together in a flash. A great choice for dessert.

Serves: 21

Time: 30 mins.

Ingredients:

- butter (¼ cup)
- mini marshmallows (1 bag (10.5 oz), plus 2 cups)
- golden Graham cereal (7 cups)
- chocolate chips (2 cups)

Directions:

1. Use cooking spray to grease a 9×9 pan.

2. Melt butter over low heat.

3. Mix in the bag of marshmallows, stir frequently until totally melted. Remove and set aside.

4. Mix in the 7 cups of Graham cereal then set aside for roughly 2 minutes.

5. Now, add the 2 additional cups of marshmallows, stir until totally combined.

6. Add chocolate chips and mix in until combined. There will be a difficulty stirring the mixture at this point, and the chocolate chips will start melting slightly.

7. After mixing in the chips, pour into the prepared pan. Press evenly.

8. Let cool for at least 15 minutes before cutting into squares.

Gooey Crispy Ritz S'mores Pops

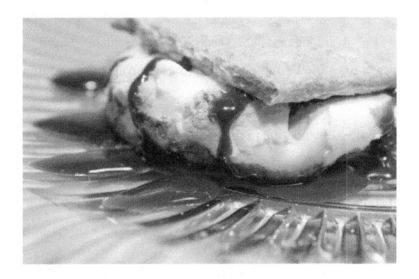

This is the perfect mix of creamy, salty, sweet and crunchy! It's very simple too because there is no baking involved.

Serves: 12

Time: 50 mins.

Ingredients:

- 1 bag marshmallows
- 14 oz. cocoa candy coating
- ½ cup graham crackers crumbs
- Lollipop sticks
- Foam or cake pop stand

Directions:

1. Insert a lollipop stick into each marshmallow.

2. Put 4 graham cracker sheets into a resealable bag and crush into fine crumbs with a mallet or a rolling pin. Dump crumbs into a bowl.

3. Melt candy coating in the microwave or in a double boiler. Dip marshmallows into coating.

4. Dip immediately into the graham cracker crumbs being sure to completely cover the marshmallow with crumb coating.

5. Insert lollipop sticks into a block of foam or on a cake pop stand and put in the refrigerator for 30 minutes to set. Alternatively, you can put a piece of parchment paper on a cookie sheet and place each lollipop on its side on the parchment paper, but this can cause the crumbs and chocolate to flake off, so the upright position is preferred.

6. Enjoy!

S'mores Whoopie Pies

An easy peasy classic s'mores treat. These delicious chocolate cookies are fused with marshmallow buttercream and graham cracker crumbs.

Serves: 10

Time: 30 mins.

Ingredients:

- butter, (½ cup, room temperature)
- light brown sugar (1 cup, packed)
- flour (1 ¼ cup)
- graham crackers (1 ½ cup, finely crushed)
- baking powder (1 ½ tsp.)
- eggs (2)
- milk (½ cup plus 2 tbsp.)
- baking soda (1 tsp.)
- vinegar (1 tsp.)
- vanilla (2 tsp.)
- Hershey Bars (6, full sized)
- Marshmallow Buttercream

Directions:

1. Preheat oven to 375 deg. F.

2. Line baking sheets with parchment paper.

3. Combine flour, graham cracker crumbs and baking powder in a suitable sized bowl. Set aside.

4. Combine milk, vinegar, vanilla and baking soda in a bowl. Stir together and set aside.

5. At medium speed, cream butter and sugar in a mixer for roughly 2 minutes. Add the eggs and continue beating until evenly incorporated.

6. On low speed, alternately add flour and milk mixture. Increase the speed to medium and beat additionally for 1 minute.

7. Drop heaped tablespoon portions onto the lined baking sheets. Place batter roughly 2 inches from each other, as the cookies spread during baking.

8. Bake 8-10 minutes until cookies are set.

9. Let cool on baking sheet for 3 minutes and then transfer to wire rack to finish cooling.

10. When all cookies are baked, melt chocolate bars in microwave on 50% power in 30 second increments, stirring after each 30 seconds. Continue until melted.

11. Flip half of the cookies over and spoon a tablespoon sized portion of melted chocolate on the bottom, spreading to the edge of the cookie.

12. Fill prepared frosting in a Ziploc or piping bag and pipe frosting on remaining cookies which are not chocolate. Leave enough space at the edge for the spreading of the frosting when it is sandwiched.

13. Use the chocolate side to top your frosting side.

14. Store for up to 5 days in an airtight container.

15. Refrigerate if desired.

Milk Chocolate S'mores Brownies

The perfect combination of two favorite desserts all in one place. Crunchy, chewy and very delicious.

Serves: 24

Time: 1 hour and 40 mins.

Ingredients:

- all-purpose flour, 1 1/3 cups
- Fluff or marshmallow crème, 1 ½ cups
- graham cracker crumbs, ¾ cup
- butter, ½ cup
- white sugar, ½ cup
- brown sugar, ¼ cup
- vanilla extract, 1 tsp.
- baking powder, 1 tsp.
- salt, ¼ tsp.
- egg, 1
- milk chocolate bars, 2, king size

Directions:

1. Preheat oven to 350 F and grease an 8x8 pan.

2. Put 6 graham cracker sheets into a resealable bag and crush into fine crumbs with a mallet or a rolling pin.

3. Whisk together flour, salt, baking powder, and graham cracker crumbs. Set aside.

4. In another bowl, cream the butter and sugar together.

5. Slowly beat the egg and vanilla into the butter and sugar mix.

6. Add the dry ingredients to the wet ingredients. Mix until a thick dough is formed.

7. Spread half of the dough mixture across the bottom of the pan.

8. Pour the marshmallow creme or Fluff on top of the dough.

9. Place the 2 chocolate bars on top of the marshmallow.

10. Fit the remaining dough over the chocolate. Enjoy!

Salty Peanut Butter S'mores Truffles

These are simple, delicious no bake treats with all the flavors of a fancy s'more packed in.

Serves: 7

Time: 30 mins.

Ingredients:

- crushed Ritz Crackers (1 ¼ cup, crushed)
- creamy peanut butter (¾ cup)
- Marshmallow Fluff (½ cup)
- mini chocolate chips (1 cup)
- milk chocolate, (8 oz., chopped)
- flaked sea salt to garnish

Directions:

1. In a suitable sized bowl, mix together the crushed crackers, Fluff, peanut butter and chocolate chips. Cover the bowl and let chill for an hour.

2. Take the bowl from the refrigerator, form the mixture into 1-inch balls. Use parchment paper to line your baking sheet and place the balls on it and put them back in the refrigerator for an additional 15 minutes.

3. In the meantime, chop the milk chocolate, melt it in the microwave at 25 seconds intervals until it is smooth.

4. Into the melted chocolate, dip balls, tap off the excess chocolate then return to the lined baking sheet. While the chocolate is still wet, sprinkle with sea salt.

5. Return the truffles to the refrigerator until chocolate is set.

6. Serve chilled or at room temperature.

Dirty S'mores Cookies

These sweet cookies are simple, chewy, they are coated in Graham crackers to make them a bit dirty.

Serves: 18

Time: 30 mins.

Ingredients:

- 1 cup butter, cold cubed
- 1 ¼ cups light brown sugar
- 1 egg plus 1 yolk
- 2 teaspoons vanilla
- ¾ teaspoon kosher salt
- 1 teaspoon baking soda
- 2 ½ cups flour
- 2 cups milk chocolate chips
- 1 (3 ounce) container Marshmallow Bits
- 1 cup graham cracker crumbs

Directions:

1. Combine your sugar and butter in your stand mixture and beat with a paddle on medium until fluffy (about 2 mins).

2. Add the egg, yolk, vanilla, salt and baking soda and continue mixing for 1 more minute until smooth, scraping the sides of the bowl as necessary.

3. Switch to a low speed then add in the flour then mix until fully combined.

4. With mixer still on low add in the chocolate chips and marshmallow bits until evenly incorporated.

5. Cover the dough and chill it in the refrigerator for at least an hour.

6. Preheat the oven to 350°F.

7. Line a baking sheet with parchment paper. Scoop out 2 tablespoons of the cookie dough and roll it into a ball. Use the graham cracker crumbs to cover each ball evenly.

8. Place the dough onto the baking sheet 2- inches apart and bake for 9-10 minutes until the edges are lightly golden.

9. Allow the cookies to cool on the baking sheet for 3 minutes before transferring them to a wire rack to cool completely.

S'mores Cupcakes

Really moist cupcake with Graham cracker crust. A real tasty treat.

Serves: 24

Time: 40 mins.

Ingredients:

- chocolate cake mix (1 box)
- graham crackers (1 ½ cups, crushed)
- sugar (¼ cup)
- butter (5 tbsp., melted)
- Hershey's Milk Chocolate Bars (6, full sized)
- mini marshmallows (2 cups, for garnish)
- Marshmallow Buttercream (double batch)

Directions:

1. Heat oven to 350 degrees F.

2. Use cupcake liners to line 2 (12 cups) muffin tins.

3. In a suitable sized bowl, add sugar, Graham cracker crumbs sugar and melted butter, combine. Drop a tablespoon of the cracker mixture into each of the muffin cup, pressing down to form a crust.

4. Allow roughly 5 minutes for baking the crust. Transfer to wire rack upon completion.

5. Prepare cake mix according to package directions. Fill liners 2/3 full.

6. Bake 15-20 minutes, until cupcakes are set.

7. Break small pieces of Hershey's bars and melt in the microwave, for 30 seconds on 50% power, stirring in every 30 seconds. Repeat until they are all melted.

8. Spoon a tablespoon of chocolate on the top of each cupcake, spreading to cover.

9. Set the cupcakes to chill until chocolate is set.

10. Make a double batch of Marshmallow Buttercream

11. When chocolate is set, frost cupcakes.

12. If desired, drizzle with chocolate remaining chocolate. (you might need to reheat)

13. Next, spread marshmallows on a baking sheet for toasting. Set oven to broil.

14. When oven is hot and ready, place the baking sheet on the top rack. The marshmallows toast very quickly, so toast them for 15 SECONDS under broiler. Stay close.

15. Remove from the oven, then garnish cupcakes.

S'mores Cheesecake

A mouth-watering S'mores Cheesecake, very rich and decadent.

Serves: 16

Time: 45 mins.

Ingredients:

Crust:

- graham crackers crumbs (2 ½ cups)
- granulated sugar (½ cup)
- butter (¾ cup, melted)
- mini marshmallows (2 cups)
- hot fudge ice cream topping (½ cup, warmed)

Cheesecake:

- cream cheese (16 oz., room temperature)
- sweetened condensed milk (14 oz.)
- vanilla (2 tsp.)
- 3 eggs
- mini chocolate chips (1 cup)
- mini marshmallows (2 ½ cups, divided)

Garnish:

- Hershey bars (2, broken into pieces)
- graham cracker crumbs (¼ cup)
- Hot Fudge Sauce (¼ to ½ cup)

Directions:

1. Set your oven to preheat to 325 degrees F.

Crust

2. Combine your butter, graham crackers and granulated sugar in a bowl. Transfer your mixture to a 10-inch springform pan and press evenly to form a crust.

3. Top your crust evenly with your crust portion of mini marshmallows then drizzle with warmed hot fudge. Set aside.

Cheesecake

4. Combine your condensed milk and cream cheese in your stand mixer. Process on low for about 3 minutes (until smooth).

5. Add your vanilla then eggs, one at a time. Be careful not to over-mix.

6. Add your chocolate chips and stir. Once combined add in a cup of mini marshmallows.

7. Transfer your mixture over the crust.

8. Set to bake until set (about 45 minutes). Once done, top with the remaining marshmallows. Return to the oven until golden and puffed (about 5 minutes).

9. Set to cool on a wire rack (about 30 minutes). Drop the cake out of the pan by loosening the sides of the springform pan. Cover and set to cool in the refrigerator overnight.

10. Sprinkle with additional graham crumbs, Hershey bars then drizzle with hot fudge.

11. Serve and enjoy!

Chocolate Chip Cookie Peanut Butter S'mores Bars

This delicious smore cookie will take you back to the camp fire.

Serves: 12

Time: 30 mins.

Ingredients:

- Cookie dough (32 oz., pre-made)
- Chocolate Bars (16 oz, Milk Chocolate, Hershey)
- peanut butter (1 cup, creamy)
- graham cracker crumbs (½ cup)
- Marshmallow fluff (1 ½ cups)

Directions:

1. Set your oven to preheat to 350°F and prepare a 9x9 pan by lining with foil then coating lightly with oil.

2. Press 25oz. of your cookie dough into the base of your pan then top with your chocolate bars.

3. Using a knife or off-set spatula, top evenly with your peanut butter.

4. Sprinkle your cracker crumbs on top of the peanut butter then cover evenly with marshmallow fluff.

5. Lightly dust your counter to with flour then carefully roll out the remainder of your cookie dough. Fit your rolled cookie dough on top of the fluff.

6. Set to bake until golden (about 22 minutes).

7. Place on a wire rack to cool for about 2 hours before transferring to refrigerator for another 2 hours.

8. Cut into squares then serve.

Skillet S'mores Cookie

This cookie is moist, tender and tasty.

Serves: 10

Time: 30 mins.

Ingredients:

- butter (1 cup, room temperature)
- brown sugar (1 ½ cups)
- eggs (2)
- vanilla (2 tsp)
- baking soda (1 tsp)
- kosher salt (1 tsp)
- graham cracker crumbs (1 ½ cups)
- flour (2 ¼ cups)
- Milk Chocolate Bars (2 cups, chopped)
- mini marshmallow (1 ½ cups)
- Marshmallows (8 – 9, giant, cut in thirds)

Directions:

1. Set the oven to preheat to 350°F.

2. Place your sugar and butter in a stand mixer bowl and beat until fluffy and light (about 2 minutes).

3. Add in eggs and vanilla and mix until evenly combined, scraping sides as needed.

4. Mix in your salt and baking soda. Once incorporated add in your cracker crumbs, flour, then chopped milk chocolate.

5. Transfer a half of your dough into a skillet then add in your mini marshmallows. Use your remaining dough to cover the marshmallows.

6. Set to bake for 15 minutes.

7. Once the times elapsed, cover with giant marshmallows then return to bake until golden (about 10 minutes).

8. Serve warm and enjoy.

Chocolate Chip Peanut Butter S'mores

These delicious smores are sweet, chewy and easy to whip up.

Serves: 4

Time: 30 mins.

Ingredients:

- Cookies (8, chocolate chip)
- peanut butter (2 tablespoons, creamy)
- chocolate (4 square, dark)
- marshmallows (4, vanilla bean)

Directions:

1. Spread your peanut butter evenly on the inside of 4 cookies.

2. Top with a chocolate square then add a marshmallow on top.

3. Set your broiler to preheat to high.

4. Place your cookies beneath the broiler to broil until golden and bubbly (about 2 minutes)

5. Once done, top with the remaining set of cookies.

Devil's Food S'mores Cupcakes

This delicious recipe is the perfect mix between Devil's Food Cake and a Smore.

Serves: 24

Time: 40 mins.

Ingredients:

- Devil's Food cake mix (1 box)
- graham crackers (1 ½ cups, crushed)
- sugar (¼ cup)
- butter (5 tbsp., melted)
- Hershey's Milk Chocolate Bars (6, full sized)
- mini marshmallows (2 cups, for garnish)
- Marshmallow Buttercream (double batch)

Directions:

1. Heat oven to 350 degrees F.

2. Use cupcake liners to line 2 (12 cups) muffin tins.

3. In a suitable sized bowl, add sugar, Graham cracker crumbs sugar and melted butter, combine. Drop a tablespoon of the cracker mixture into each of the muffin cup, pressing down to form a crust.

4. Allow roughly 5 minutes for baking the crust. Transfer to wire rack upon completion.

5. Prepare cake mix according to package directions. Fill liners 2/3 full.

6. Bake 15-20 minutes, until cupcakes are set.

7. Break small pieces of Hershey's bars and melt in microwave, 30 seconds on 50% power, stirring after every 30 seconds. Repeat until melted.

8. Top with a spoon of chocolate, spread and place the cupcakes to set in the fridge.

9. Make a double batch of Marshmallow Buttercream

10. When chocolate is set, frost cupcakes.

11. If desired, drizzle with chocolate remaining chocolate. (you might need to reheat)

12. Next, spread marshmallows on a baking sheet for toasting. Set oven to broil.

13. When oven is hot and ready, place the baking sheet on the top rack. The marshmallows toast very quickly, so toast them for 15 SECONDS under broiler. Stay close.

14. Remove from the oven, then garnish cupcakes.

No Bake S'mores Cheesecakes

Thes tasty smores can be whip up for any day of the week without even touching the oven.

Serves: 2

Time: 6 hours 30 minutes

Ingredients:

Crust Topping:

- 4 tbsp. unsalted butter, melted
- 2/3 c. graham cracker crumbs
- ½ c. marshmallow fluff or cream
- 4 marshmallows, toasted and cut in half

Chocolate Ganache:

- 4 oz. milk chocolate, chopped
- 3 tbsp. heavy cream
- Marshmallow Cheesecake:
- cream cheese, ½ c., whipped
- ½ c. marshmallow fluff or cream
- 1/3 c. sweetened condensed milk
- 2 teaspoons vanilla extract

Directions:

1. In a small bowl, combine your graham crumbs and butter until moistened.

2. Create a crust by pressing your crumb mixture into your ramekin with a spoon.

3. Place the chocolate in a bowl.

4. Set your heavy cream to warm in a saucepan on medium heat until it simmers.

5. Add your warmed cream on top of the chocolate then allow to rest for a few seconds before stirring to allow the chocolate to fully melt, and combine.

6. Add about a teaspoon of ganache on the top of each graham crust.

7. Beat the cream cheese in the bowl of your electric mixer on the medium speed until creamy.

8. Add in your fluff then continue to beat until fully combined. On a low speed, beat in your vanilla and milk.

9. Beat on the high speed until a smooth batter forms.

10. Use the batter to top your chocolate ganache, leaving space on top for more chocolate and marshmallow.

11. Add another teaspoon of the ganache on the top of cheesecake and a sprinkle of graham crumbs if you want, then refrigerate for 4- 6 hours.

12. When ready to serve, add a tbsp. of marshmallow fluff on the top of ganache, then top it with a toasted marshmallow.

13. Top with additional graham crumbs then serve!

14. Enjoy!

S'More Cereal Treats

These tasty cereal treats for perfect for midday snacks.

Serves: 8

Time: 30 mins.

Ingredients:

- 3 cups chocolate rice cereal
- 3 cups honey graham cereal
- 1 cup chocolate chips
- ¼ cup butter
- 1 bag of marshmallows

Directions:

1. In a saucepan, melt the butter on medium heat. Add marshmallows. Stir and heat until a marshmallow sauce is formed.

2. Add in both cereals.

3. Stir in chocolate chips.

4. Press into a greased 9x13 pan. Cut into squares.

5. Enjoy!

S'More Croissants

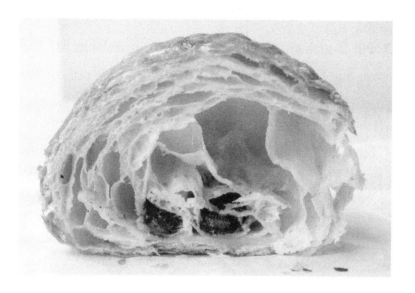

These smore croissants are perfect for an afternoon picnic.

Serves: 6

Time: 30 mins.

Ingredients:

- 1 package crescent rolls
- 1 bag mini marshmallows
- ¼ cup graham cracker crumbs
- ½ cup mini chocolate chips

Directions:

1. Unpackage crescent rolls and lay them out as triangles.

2. Put 2 graham cracker sheets into a resealable bag and crush into fine crumbs with a mallet or a rolling pin.

3. Sprinkle the crumbs onto each crescent roll.

4. Put chocolate chips and mini marshmallows in the center of each triangle.

5. Roll up the dough into crescent rolls.

6. Bake as directed on the roll packaging. Enjoy!

S'More Snack Mix

For a quick and tasty snack for the kids or the young at heart, enjoy a serving of this tasty smore snack mix.

Serves: 6

Time: 30 mins.

Ingredients:

- 6 cups honey graham cereal
- 2 ½ cups mini marshmallows
- 1 ½ cups chocolate chips
- ¾ cup light corn syrup
- 3 tablespoons butter
- 1 teaspoon vanilla

Directions:

1. Grease a cookie sheet.

2. Combine chocolate chips, corn syrup, and butter in a saucepan over medium heat. Stir occasionally.

3. Remove from heat when chocolate is melted and add vanilla.

4. In a separate bowl toss cereal and marshmallows.

5. Pour chocolate mixture over the cereal and marshmallows.

6. Pour onto the cookie sheet and press down slightly on the mixture with your palm.

7. Let set for an hour and then break into bite size clusters. Enjoy!

S'More Candy Bars

Sweet, gooey and perfect.

Serves: 8

Time: 30 mins. + Setting time

Ingredients:

- 14 oz. cocoa candy melt
- 7.5 oz jar of Fluff or 2 ½ cups marshmallow creme
- 8 graham cracker sheets
- Candy bar molds or aluminum foil and parchment paper

Directions:

1. If you don't have candy molds that will fit one graham cracker, break off one graham cracker from the sheet and shape the aluminum foil around it to make your own mold. Place parchment paper at the bottom.

2. If you prefer to make a king size candy bar, shape your mold around one whole sheet of graham crackers.

3. Melt the candy coating in a double boiler or in the microwave.

4. Pour half the chocolate into each mold. Put the other half aside.

5. Spread Fluff or marshmallow creme on each graham cracker.

6. Place graham cracker, Fluff side down into the chocolate.

7. Pour the rest of the chocolate on top of the graham cracker.

8. Let chocolate set. Enjoy!

S'More Pizza

Pizzas can be sweet too. Enjoy this sweet smore pizza in a matter of minutes with your entire family.

Serves: 6

Time: 25 mins.

Ingredients:

- 3 cups marshmallows
- 2 tablespoons butter
- 1 tablespoons cinnamon
- 6 graham cracker sheets
- 2 king size chocolate bars
- 1 package of pizza dough

Directions:

1. Preheat oven to 400 F.

2. Melt butter in the microwave or in a sauce pan.

3. Roll out pizza dough. This treat is best enjoyed with a thin crust so really take the time to thin it out.

4. Brush the butter on the crust and then sprinkle with cinnamon.

5. Break the graham crackers and chocolate into bite size pieces.

6. Spread the graham crackers, chocolate, and marshmallows around the pizza.

7. Bake for 11 minutes on a cookie sheet or pizza stone or until marshmallows are browned.

S'More Stuffed Brownies

These delicious brownies are moist, easy to whip up and tender.

Serves: 12

Time: 45 mins.

Ingredients:

- white sugar, 2 c.
- flour, 1 c., all-purpose
- butter, 1 c.
- cocoa powder, ½ c., unsweetened
- vanilla extract, 1 tsp.
- baking powder, ½ tsp.
- salt, ½ tsp.
- eggs, 4
- graham cracker, 6 sheets
- marshmallows, 16
- chocolate bars, 2, large

Directions:

1. Set your oven to preheat to 350 F and grease 9x13 pan.

2. Sift flour, cocoa powder, baking powder, and salt into a bowl. Set aside.

3. Cream sugar and softened butter. Mix in vanilla and eggs.

4. Add the ingredients from step 2 into the wet mixture. Mix until smooth.

5. Pour half the batter into the pan.

6. Layer graham crackers onto batter. Follow with marshmallows and then chocolate.

7. Pour the second half of the batter on top.

8. Bake for 30-35 minutes.

9. Cut into brownies. Enjoy!

S'Moretini

For a sweet, tasty dessert drink, give this S'moretini recipe a try.

Serves: 2

Time: 15 mins.

Ingredients:

- 2 oz. heavy cream
- 1 oz. vanilla vodka
- 1 oz. chocolate vodka
- 1 oz. Irish Cream
- 1 oz. chocolate liqueur
- 1 crushed graham cracker sheet
- Chocolate syrup to rim the glass

Directions:

Put a graham cracker sheet into a resealable bag and crush into fine crumbs with a mallet or a rolling pin.

Dip martini glass into chocolate syrup. Follow by dipping in graham cracker crumbs.

Put in fridge to set the garnished rim.

Mix heavy cream, vodkas, Irish cream, and liqueur in a martini shaker filled with ice.

Pour into chilled martini glasses. Enjoy!

After Dinner S'More Coffee Liqueur

Here we have yet another dessert drink that is quick to whip up and extremely delicious.

Serves: 2

Time: 15 mins.

Ingredients:

- 4 oz. coffee, prepared
- 2 oz. chocolate liqueur
- 1 oz. Irish cream
- 1 oz. rum
- 1 tablespoon Fluff or marshmallow creme
- 1 crushed graham cracker sheet

Directions:

1. Put a graham cracker sheet into a resealable bag and crush into fine crumbs with a mallet or a rolling pin.

2. Mix coffee, chocolate liqueur, and rum in a mug.

3. Mix together Fluff and Irish Cream. Add to coffee.

4. Sprinkle with graham cracker crumbs to garnish. Enjoy!

Extra Thick S'More Shake

This smore milkshake will blow your mind. Enjoy it as either a evening snack or dessert.

Serves: 2

Time: 15 mins.

Ingredients:

- 1 ½ cups chocolate ice cream
- ½ cup whole milk
- ¼ cup heavy cream
- ¼ cup Fluff or marshmallow creme
- 1/8 cup chocolate syrup
- 1 crushed graham cracker sheet

Directions:

1. Stick heavy cream in the freezer for 5 minutes before using.

2. Put a graham cracker sheet into a resealable bag and crush into fine crumbs with a mallet or a rolling pin.

3. Whip together heavy cream and Fluff or marshmallow creme.

4. In a blender, mix chocolate ice cream, milk, and chocolate syrup.

5. Layer whipped marshmallow and chocolate milkshake in 2 tall glasses.

6. Garnish with graham cracker crumbs. Enjoy!

No Bake S'More Bars

These bars are gooey, sweet and delicious.

Serves: 8

Time: 6 hours 20 mins.

Ingredients:

- 1 ½ cups graham cracker crumbs
- 1 cup chocolate chips
- ¾ cup of Fluff or marshmallow creme
- ¼ cup white sugar
- 2 ½ tablespoons unsalted butter

Directions:

1. Line an 8x8 pan with parchment paper.

2. Put 12 graham cracker sheets into a resealable bag and crush into fine crumbs with a mallet or a rolling pin.

3. Melt butter in a saucepan or microwave.

4. Mix together crumbs, butter, and sugar to form a crust. Press into the bottom of the pan.

5. Melt chocolate in a double boiler or microwave.

6. Pour chocolate on top of graham cracker crust. Allow to cool for a few minutes.

7. Spoon out Fluff or marshmallow creme on top of the chocolate.

8. With a knife swirl the chocolate and marshmallow together.

9. Let set in the refrigerator for 6 hours.

10. Cut into square bars. Enjoy!

No Bake S'More Balls

If you are seeking a quick and easy snack to whip up, these smore balls will rock your world.

Serves: 10

Time: 20 mins.

Ingredients:

- graham cracker crumbs, ¾ cup
- mini-marshmallows, ½ cup
- peanut butter, 1/3 cup
- chocolate syrup, ¼ cup
- mini-chocolate chips, ¼ cup
- golden syrup, 2 tablespoons
- oats, 2 tablespoons

Directions:

1. Put 6 graham cracker sheets into a resealable bag and crush into fine crumbs with a mallet or a rolling pin.

2. Mix graham cracker crumbs, peanut butter, oats, chocolate syrup, and golden syrup.

3. Spoon dough onto a cookie sheet and then flatten into silver dollar size dough with your palm.

4. Add a mini-marshmallow and a few mini-chocolate chips to each piece of dough.

5. Surround the marshmallow and chocolate chips with dough and roll into a ball. Enjoy!

S'mores No-Bake Cookies

Very simple, very tasty. Just mix together and chill until you are ready to serve.

Serves: 12

Time: 30 mins.

Ingredients:

- butter (¼ cup)
- mini marshmallows (10.5 oz. bag)
- milk chocolate chips (11.5 oz. bag)
- chips (1 cup, for drizzling) optional
- Golden Graham cereal (8 cups)

Directions:

1. Over medium heat in a medium-sized stockpot, melt butter.

2. Next, add the marshmallows stirring constantly until melted. Take off heat.

3. Stir in the cereal until well coated.

4. Add in the chocolate chips and stir constantly until distributed evenly. (If you prefer not to have the chips melt much, freeze them beforehand.)

5. Shape the mixture into small clumps using a spoon. Place on wax or parchment paper to cool.

6. If using the drizzle, use a double-boiler to melt the chocolate chips or melt in the microwave (carefully).

7. If the chocolate is a bit too thick, stir in a teaspoon or two of shortening or vegetable oil to thin.

8. Transfer the melted chocolate to a pastry bag fitted with a small tip, use to drizzle onto the cookies once they have slightly cooled.

9. If you do not have a pastry bag, a Ziploc bag can be used (just snip a tiny piece off at a corner to drizzle.

10. Enjoy!

Chocolate Stout S'Mores Bars

Camping just is not the same without these chewy, crunchy, gooey treats of campfire s'mores.

Serves: 6

Time: 45 mins.

Ingredients:

- graham crackers (10 pcs.)
- standard size marshmallows (3 cups)
- butter (3 tbsp., melted)
- chocolate stout (¾ cup)
- brown sugar (2 tbs.)
- flour (½ cup)
- 3 eggs
- butter (1 stick)
- white sugar (1 cup)
- salt (½ tsp)
- brown sugar (½ cup)
- cocoa powder (1 cup)
- dark chocolate chips (½ cup)

Directions:

1. Heat oven to 350 degrees F.

2. Place the graham crackers and the brown sugar in a food processor. Process until crumbled.

3. Remove the stopper out of the food processor lid.

4. While the food processor is on, add 3 tbsp. melted butter slowly. Pulse until it resembles wet sand.

5. Add to a 9 x 13 pan.

6. Distribute mixture evenly along the bottom. Press firmly into place.

7. In a suitable container, beat on high speed the eggs and both sugars until well combined. Beat for roughly 3 minutes.

8. Place the butter and chocolate chips in a microwavable safe bowl.

9. Microwave for 30 seconds on high. Stir repeatedly until melted and thoroughly combined.

10. Beat the chocolate in the egg/sugar mixture until well combined.

11. In another bowl, mix the salt, cocoa powder and the flour until thoroughly combined.

12. Add to the wet ingredients and then stir until just combined.

13. Pour the batter over the crust.

14. Place the marshmallows evenly across the top, ensuring a half inch border is left along the edge.

15. Bake at 350 degrees for 22 minutes or until the marshmallows are golden brown.

16. You still want the bars to be soft, don't over bake them, they will continue to set as they cool.

17. Enjoy!

No-Bake S'mores Pie

This is a great summer dessert especially when you can't be bothered to turn on the oven. It is a rich, creamy and sweet no-bake dessert.

Serves: 12

Time: 2 hours

Ingredients:

For the Crust:

- graham cracker crumbs (1 ½ cup)
- malted milk powder (¼ cup)
- granulated sugar (2 tbsp.)
- kosher salt (¾ tsp.)
- unsalted butter (¼ cup, melted)
- heavy cream (¼ cup)

For the Chocolate Filling:

- bittersweet chocolate (8 oz., finely chopped)
- heavy cream (¼ cup)
- light corn syrup (1 ½ tsp.)
- unsalted butter (2 ½ tbsp.)

For the Marshmallow Topping:

- marshmallows (10 oz.)

Directions:

Make the Graham Cracker Crust:

1. In a large bowl, whisk together the malted milk powder, graham cracker crumbs, salt and sugar.

2. In a measuring cup, whisk together the heavy cream and melted butter then pour over the crumb mixture.

3. Using a rubber spatula, fold the ingredients and mix together until all the dry ingredients are evenly moistened.

4. Place the mixture into a 9-inch pie dish, pressing evenly along the bottom and up the sides of the dish.

5. Refrigerate while the chocolate filling is prepared.

Make the Chocolate Filling:

1. Place the chopped chocolate in a medium bowl.

2. Then mix the corn syrup and heavy cream in a small saucepan and place over the medium heat. Warm until it just barely starts boiling.

3. Remove mixture from the heat, then pour over the chopped chocolate.

4. Set aside for 1 minute. Stir gently with a spatula until the chocolate is thoroughly melted and combined.

5. Add the butter and stir until it is melted and incorporated. (microwave in 10-second slots on 50 per cent power if the mixture cools down too much to totally melt the chocolate or butter. Stir until all is completely melted.)

6. Pour the chocolate mixture in to the chilled pie crust and spread into an even layer.

7. Press the marshmallows gently into the chocolate filling, covering the top of the pie with the marshmallows.

8. Chill the pie briefly (30 minutes to 60 minutes) to allow the chocolate the set.

9. When ready to serve, use your kitchen torch to toast the marshmallows.

10. The pie can be kept at the room temperature providing it's not warmer than about 72 degrees.

11. If your kitchen is warmer than that, then I recommend refrigerating the pie, so the chocolate filling does not melt.

12. Enjoy!

Chocolate Glaze S'mores Cupcakes

Delight yourself in every bite of these decadent smore cupcakes.

Serves: 12

Time: 1 hour

Ingredients:

- Graham Cracker Layer:
- graham cracker crumbs (1 ½ cups)
- butter melted Chocolate (7 tbsp.)
- all-purpose flour (1 cup)
- sugar (1 cup plus 2 tbsp.)
- Unsweetened Natural Cocoa Powder (1/3 cup plus 2 tbsp.)
- baking soda (½ tsp.)
- salt (¼ tsp.)
- unsalted butter (½ cup, melted and warm)
- eggs (2 large)
- pure vanilla extract (1 tsp.)
- instant coffee (2 tbsp.)
- hot coffee (½ cup)
- Marshmallow Frosting
- egg whites (5 large)
- cup sugar (1 ½ cup)
- Chocolate Glaze:
- dark chocolate (2/3 cup)
- heavy cream (2 tbsp.)
- powdered sugar (4 tbsp., sifted)
- water (4 to 5 tbsp., warm)

Directions:

1. Heat oven to 350 degrees F. Place a rack in the lower third of the oven. Line muffin tin with parchment paper.

Graham Cracker Layer:

2. Reserve 2 tablespoons of crumbs. Place remaining crumbs in a bowl with the butter and mix together.

3. Add approximately 1 tablespoon of mixture to each lined cup and press crumbs down firmly.

4. Bake for roughly 10- 12 minutes.

To Make Cupcake:

1. Add to a bowl flour, sugar, baking soda, cocoa powder, sugar and salt, mix thoroughly to combine.

2. Add butter, eggs, and vanilla. Beat at medium speed for approximately one minute. Add in the coffee granules and beat for 30 seconds or until the batter is smooth. The batter should be thin enough to pour.

3. Evenly divide it among the graham cracker cups.

4. Bake for roughly 18-22 minutes just until a toothpick put into a few of the cupcakes has come out clean.

5. Set the pan to cool on a rack.

6. When the cupcakes are completely cool, they can be frosted.

7. Enjoy!

Thin Mint Girl Scout Cookie S'mores

This recipe is a real Girl Scout summer treat.

Serves: 4

Time: 15 mins.

Ingredients:

- 4 marshmallows (large campfire)
- 8 honey graham crackers
- 1 chocolate bar (broken into halves)
- 4 Girl Scout Cookies (thin mint)

Directions:

1. Roast marshmallows.

2. Add a chocolate bar on a graham cracker.

3. Top with a thin mint then sandwich the roasted marshmallow between them.

4. Enjoy!

S'mores Milkshake

A cool dessert for you. A refreshing ice-cream milkshake which is s'more in liquid form packed with toasted marshmallows and crackers.

Serves: 2

Time: 10 minutes

Ingredients:

- Vanilla Ice Cream (packed)
- Milk
- large Marshmallows (toasted)
- regular Graham Crackers (2 sheets)
- chocolate hazelnut spread (¼ cup)

Directions:

1. In a blender, place desired amount of milk.

2. Add in the ice cream. Blend until smooth.

3. Add toasted marshmallows, hazelnut spread and graham crackers.

4. Pulse until all ingredients are incorporated.

5. Enjoy!

Conclusion

You did it! Congrats, on making it to end of this Smore Cookbook with us. We hope you had fun practicing all 30 delicious smore recipes that are perfect for any time of day.

So, what's next?

Practice becomes perfect. So, keep on enjoying new and exciting meals with your whole family. Then whenever you are ready for another spark of delicious inspiration grab another one of our books and let us continue your culinary journey together.

Remember, drop us a review if you loved what you read and until we meet again, keep on cooking delicious food.

About the Author

Born in New Germantown, Pennsylvania, Stephanie Sharp received a Masters degree from Penn State in English Literature. Driven by her passion to create culinary masterpieces, she applied and was accepted to The International Culinary School of the Art Institute where she excelled in French cuisine. She has married her cooking skills with an aptitude for business by opening her own small cooking school where she teaches students of all ages.

Stephanie's talents extend to being an author as well and she has written over 400 e-books on the art of cooking and baking that include her most popular recipes.

Sharp has been fortunate enough to raise a family near her hometown in Pennsylvania where she, her husband and children live in a beautiful rustic house on an extensive piece of land. Her other passion is taking care of the furry members of her family which include 3 cats, 2 dogs and a potbelly pig named Wilbur.

Watch for more amazing books by Stephanie Sharp coming out in the next few months.

Author's Afterthoughts

I am truly grateful to you for taking the time to read my book. I cherish all of my readers! Thanks ever so much to each of my cherished readers for investing the time to read this book!

With so many options available to you, your choice to buy my book is an honour, so my heartfelt thanks at reading it from beginning to end!

I value your feedback, so please take a moment to submit an honest and open review on Amazon so I can get valuable insight into my readers' opinions and others can benefit from your experience.

Thank you for taking the time to review!

Stephanie Sharp

For announcements about new releases, please

follow my author page on Amazon.com!

(Look for the Follow Bottom under the photo)

You can find that at:

https://www.amazon.com/author/stephanie-sharp

*or Scan **QR-code** below.*